Augustus R. Buckland

The Heroic in Missions

Pioneers in six fields

Augustus R. Buckland

The Heroic in Missions
Pioneers in six fields

ISBN/EAN: 9783337193379

Printed in Europe, USA, Canada, Australia, Japan

Cover: Foto ©Andreas Hilbeck / pixelio.de

More available books at **www.hansebooks.com**

THE HEROIC IN MISSIONS

THE
HEROIC IN MISSIONS

PIONEERS IN SIX FIELDS

BY

THE REV. AUGUSTUS R. BUCKLAND M.A.

MORNING PREACHER AT THE FOUNDLING HOSPITAL

NEW YORK
THOMAS WHITTAKER
2 & 3 BIBLE HOUSE
1894

CONTENTS

CHAP.		PAGE
I.	THE HEROISM OF PATIENCE	7
II.	THE PIONEER IN JAPAN	25
III.	THE GRAVES BY THE VICTORIA NYANZA	43
IV.	A PIONEER IN THE FAR WEST	61
V.	THE PILGRIM MISSIONARY OF THE PUNJAB	81
VI.	THE MEN WHO DIED AT LOKOJA	97

" ' Ill and o'erworked, how fare you in this scene ? '
' Bravely,' said he, ' for I of late have been
Much cheered with thoughts of Christ, the Living Bread.'
O human soul ! as long as thou canst so
Set up a mark of everlasting light
Above the howling senses' ebb and flow,
To cheer thee, and to right thee if thou roam,
Not with lost toil thou labourest through the night !
Thou mak'st the heaven thou hop'st indeed thy home."

         MATTHEW ARNOLD.

THE HEROISM OF PATIENCE

THE HEROISM OF PATIENCE

Few things are more remarkable or more welcome than the recent increase of interest in foreign missions. Measured by any known test, that increase is striking. Though the need of more recruits is everywhere urgent, the best and noblest of men and women now give themselves to the work in numbers few would have dared to look for twenty years ago. The funds contributed, if still miserably disproportionate to our national wealth, our national savings, or our national responsibilities, must nevertheless be deemed large. And public opinion, represented by the press, has veered round in favour of the missionary. Once it was the fashion to write of the work and its agents with undisguised contempt. Sometimes charity allowed the missionary to be dismissed as a mere fanatic; but not seldom his motives were impugned, his aims misrepresented, and his life caricatured for the entertainment of all observers. There has been of late a slight recrudescence of these outrages. But it is only a witness to the success of a movement which challenges at every step the hostility of the cynical rationalist or of the nominal Christian. It may serve also to remind us that sometimes a missionary society exhibits its mere humanity by making a mistake. It chooses the wrong man, and the wrong man brings discredit on his class.

Events have favoured the cause. The devotion of a little band who went out to China with Mr. C. T. Studd and Mr. Stanley Smith stirred inquiry in quarters where missionary enterprise may have been regarded as the proper pursuit of the weakling rather than of the men who had taken the highest honours on the cricket-field and the river. The murder of Bishop Hannington and the frightful persecution of the young converts in Uganda repeated the martyr triumphs of apostolic days. The death of James Gilmour called to his countrymen's mind the courage of the pioneer who braved the perils of an attempt to evangelise the Mongols. The loss of Alexander

Mackay in his dogged hoping and waiting and working for better times around the Victoria Nyanza; the wonderful records of peril and preservation which we have learned to associate with the name of John G. Paton; the eloquence of such deaths as those of Bishop French, essaying single-handed new fields in his old age, or of J. Alfred Robinson and Graham Wilmot Brooke, resigning all to live a little while and then to die by the waters of the Niger—these things, coming to a generation which has not forgotten Livingstone, or Moffat, or Patteson, have left their mark perceptibly upon it.

There is still much to be done. It is something to get the work known in the circle of its intimate friends; but it is well to make the interest more general, to carry the intelligence beyond the limits of subscribers' homes, and to deliver it as news from the front to all who claim part or lot in the Church of Christ. In view of this no apology is needed for an attempt once more to illustrate the heroic side of missionary enterprise. The illustrations are taken from the work of one organisation to give the story greater coherence, and not from any belief that the history of the

Church Missionary Society is distinguished above that of all other agencies in this particular.

Let us begin with the Heroism of Patience. It is the heroism which the world is least disposed to recognise, but it tries the soul most. It was the capacity to stand "hard pounding" which won Waterloo. The same endurance is needed in the mission-field. At home there sit subscribers, waiting, sometimes too exactingly, to hear of triumphs. At home there sit the critics, who have put a price upon the conversion of a soul and are prepared to tell you whether it is cheap or dear. In the field the worker is face to face with natures that seem utterly unlike the natures he has known; with prejudices, compacted by the usage of generations, which laugh to scorn the advent of one man with a message; with the hostility of priests, of temple-servers, the ministers of idolatry and of superstition; with the foe within—physical depression, mental distress, even doubt as to the purpose and favour of God.

In almost every field worked by the Church Missionary Society the heroism of patience has been called for. In Sierra Leone, when the century was young, fifteen missionaries and eleven wives had reached the field, and fifteen of the twenty-six had died before the first convert was baptised by Edward Bickersteth. On Christmas Day 1814—the very day whereon the first Indian bishop preached his first sermon in Calcutta—Samuel Marsden opened the Church Missionary Society's work amongst the Maories. It was eleven years before one convert came in, and five years again before others followed. The earliest attempt to reach the Gonds of India was made in 1835. The work was re-organised, after intervals, in 1879; but it was not till 1885 that the first-fruits were gathered. The Fuh-Kien mission was planted in 1850; there were no baptisms until 1861. The remnant of the pioneer mission to Uganda reached the capital in 1877. Not until 1882 were the first five converts welcomed. It would be easy to extend the list; but instead, let us illustrate the heroism of patience more fully by the history of Fuh-Kien.

The exponents of missionary enterprise are sometimes told that they mistake their opportunities; that they should confine themselves to the gentler races of heathendom, and to those whose worship, such as it is, condemns the faithful to a life of apprehension or of vice, rather than to the Mohammedan, the Buddhist, or the follower of Confucius. The proposal would be excellent if all religions were equally matters of mere human speculation, and every man might safely choose as temperament or surroundings suggested. But the Christian is not a free agent. He is charged with the responsibility of a message to the world, and he may not select the easiest places whereat to deliver it. The same spirit which carried St. Paul to Corinth, to Athens, to Rome, has compelled the missionaries to attack China and Japan, Egypt and Persia, as well as the centres of cultivated error in India.

It was in this spirit that the Committee of the Church Missionary Society resolved to enter the Chinese province of Fuh-Kien. Its area was ample, for the missionaries had a territory nearly as large as England to look on as their parish. The people were not far to seek; there were 20,000,000 of them, gentle and simple, learned and ignorant; by repute headstrong, self-reliant, turbulent; by way of faith, worshipping in the temples of Buddhism, or practising the stern austerities of Taouism, or staying their souls upon the maxims of Confucius; in their heart of hearts, caring most of all for their ancestors—and themselves.

To assault this stronghold, the Church Missionary Society chose, in 1849, two representatives. It was a small force, but composed of the right men. William Welton, a Cambridge graduate, who for twelve years had practised as a surgeon at Woodbridge, in Suffolk, was the leader. He was forty when he entered the service of the Society, an age at which few men seek the mission-field, and yet an age which, combined with experience such as Mr. Welton had enjoyed, fitted him well for a task requiring other qualities besides the ardour commonly associated with youth. Robert David Jackson— who is still, I believe, living—came from York, was trained by the Society, and ordained on reaching China. The destination of these two was the great city of Fuh-Chow, the capital of the province, in which European merchants had been, in their own quarter, familiar figures since Fuh-Chow was opened in 1844. Its walls enclosed 600,000 people, a flock large enough to content the most fervent evangelist.

The pioneers arrived in May 1850. One advantage they gained forthwith. As a concession to their nationality, they were allowed to live within the city walls. A part of a temple on Wu-shih-shan, or Blackstone Hill, was allotted to them as a residence. From their door the whole of "The Happy City" lay stretched before the eye; around it the beautiful valley of the Min; closing the view, a range of stately hills, behind which lies the black-tea district of Bohea.

Whilst wrestling with the difficulties of the language, the two pioneers were still able to do some work. Mr. Welton opened a dispensary, and so won for the cause a degree of toleration which might otherwise have been sought in vain. For the *literati*, who were strong in numbers on Blackstone Hill, observed the presence of the "foreign devils" with extreme discontent. Nor was their chagrin lessened when the common people —the same who heard Christ gladly—began to find the dispensary a real help. These came and were profited, and whilst receiving bodily aid were directed in a Chinese leaflet to the Physician of souls. The news spread, and patients of the better class soon presented themselves. It was impossible that this kind of thing should be allowed to go on. The *literati* began a system of petty molestations. The tiles were carried from the roof of the temple—a hint which has frequently been repeated during more recent troubles in China. The garden-door was removed as an equally plain suggestion. An appeal was made to the populace; and the lessee of the temple, finding himself in evil odour by reason of his bargain with the missionaries, finally sought release from his engagement. In the meantime the temple was crowded with eager applicants, and two successful operations for tumour made Mr. Welton famous. But the *literati* carried their appeal to Pekin, and, to save further trouble, the mission-station was removed to other buildings.

The first year passed. Something had been done; but of converts there was no sign. Settled, however, in new quarters, Mr. Welton still found numberless patients. But opposition was far from dead. On the ninth day of the ninth month 1851—All Saints' Day with us—a crowd of pleasure-seekers, keeping the seasonal festivities on Blackstone Hill, varied their kite-flying by an attack on the mission premises. They wrecked the place; but Mr. Welton, aided by a friendly priest, escaped their too pressing attentions. Nothing daunted, he set to work once more.

The second year passed. Mr. Welton was now alone, Mr. Jackson being removed to other work. The policy was bad, but it is ancient history now. And converts there were none. But the patient Welton still toiled on, learning the language and increasing in facility of utterance day by day.

The third year passed, and the signs were the same. Pekin was for the time against the solitary worker. He had tried to open a school, but the teachers he secured were seized, tortured, and imprisoned for no other reason than their connection with him. They could silence the native, but not the European. He ministered to their sick; in the leper village he preached Christ; he mingled with the thousands of students who flocked to the city for their examinations; he proclaimed the doctrines of Jesus in the midst of the Tartar garrison; he discoursed with the villagers outside the walls.

When four long years were gone, there were still no converts. Yet it seemed to Mr. Welton that things were ripening for a future harvest. Writing in 1854, he saw distinct signs of change in the attitude of the people. Books were now sought for eagerly; the patients treated at the dispensary became excellent tract distributors; and even the *literati* seemed less hostile. But the year 1854 passed, and still there was not a single convert to claim. The following year saw the commercial activity of Fuh-Chow much increased, and, possibly owing to the larger population drawn thither, the work at Mr. Welton's dispensary was greater than ever. The patients were estimated at 3,000, and many persons of standing so far overcame their scruples as to welcome the missionary at their own homes and listen to his message. But a polite hearing is not everything—even at home. In China it seemed to bear no immediate fruit.

For three years Mr. Welton had now been alone, but in 1855 he was joined by two recruits. The elder of these, the Rev. Matthew Fearnley, a Cambridge wrangler, now an incumbent in the diocese of Chester, had for four years served a Yorkshire curacy, when he volunteered for the mission-field. His companion, the Rev. Francis McCaw, was an Ulster man from Larne, an *alumnus* of Trinity College, Dublin, who had been five years in orders. Their first work was to learn the language; but before they were able to preach in public Mr. Welton had left the field. The long strain had at last broken him down. A visit to Shanghai was first tried, for he could not bring himself to leave China. It was ineffectual; and he sailed for England, only, however, after a brief respite, to die. To the last his heart was in the work, and a legacy of £1,500 testified to his wish that it should be continued.

The end of 1856 came, and still there were no converts. Yet the two young missionaries were gladly listened to. People eagerly sought for books containing "the doctrines of Jesus." Even in the main street a varied crowd would listen. The aged and heavy-laden would ask, "Is Jesus still alive?" The rich young man would in jest inquire, "What must we do, if we believe in Jesus?" A poor trader would advance as a conclusive objection, that Jesus, if God, should "make the rice cheaper." The native moralist would denounce the missionary as kin to the men who brought the opium. Some, who had suffered, directly or indirectly, from the use of the drug, would menace the speaker, and seek to raise a tumult. Then sorrow fell upon the workers. Mr. McCaw suffered first the loss of his wife; and in 1857 he followed her to the grave. Like Welton, he had to pass away uncheered by the thought of one accession to the fold of Christ. Mrs. Fearnley was in peril of her life, but it was not until 1859 that, on her account, Mr. Fearnley left the field.

And still there were no converts. The mission was nine years old. In some respects it had been singularly happy. But was it well to spend labour on a field that seemed so hopelessly barren? The question was already being discussed at home, and in 1860 a strong party within the Society's Committee held that the lack of fruit was so conspicuous as to show that God was calling the workers to some other field. But at this time there was in Fuh-Chow a man of Mr. Welton's spirit. George Smith was prepared for the mission-field in the Society's own college, and reached China in August 1858. Before he could speak the vernacular with ease he was at work, imperfectly, but with a zeal which even the phlegmatic Chinaman could recognise, preaching the Gospel of Christ, amidst the crowds, to individuals, to the poor, and to the *literati* up for their examinations. But fruits? None. Yet when at a Missionary Conference, to which he went, others suggested his withdrawal, Mr. Smith refused to admit the thought. "If I have to work with my hands for my daily bread, I will stop at Fuh-Chow. I believe that the Lord has much people in that city. I believe He sent me there to work for Him, and I mean to stop there." This is the faith that removes mountains. In the face of such appeals the Committee at home could not call the worker from his field. He redoubled his labours, and, in the eleventh year of the mission's existence, he was able to write home: "I hope that a brighter day is about to dawn upon us. There are three men whom I really look upon as honest inquirers." In 1861 these three and one more were baptized. But the man whose faith prevailed only lived until October 1863, and then he, too, was called away.

When Mr. Smith died at Fuh-Chow there were thirteen baptized Christians and five "catechumens." Two years later there were 35 converts; in 1868, no fewer than 227; in 1877, the adherents numbered 2,323; in 1893, they were 10,323. The mission has prospered in the numbers, in the zeal, in the fidelity of its members under persecution, as few missions have. One of Smith's successors baptized, in a few years, over 1,000 converts. The Gospel has won its way more surely in Fuh-Kien than in provinces where the first recruits were gathered in more swiftly. Perhaps it is thus that the heroism of patience finds its answer. But is it not heroism which so patiently works, waits, and hopes?

THE PIONEER IN JAPAN

THE PIONEER IN JAPAN

THE unlocking of Japan is one of the most romantic chapters in the history of the nineteenth century. But to the student of foreign missions it is all the more interesting because access to the Land of the Rising Sun has meant the opportunity of repairing a colossal blunder. To the missionary we owe the seclusion in which, for two hundred and thirty years, Japan dwelt. It was for the missionaries of a later era to show that the message of Christianity, rightly interpreted, meant no assault upon throne or constitution, but only upon faiths powerless adequately to meet the needs of men.

The task of first carrying the Gospel to Japan, when the long-closed door had been opened, was no child's-play. The dangers were many, the difficulties unique. They were not quite the same perils as confronted the few men who stood by Samuel Marsden's side in New Zealand. They differed from the insidious and too often fatal assaults which inflicted such crushing loss upon the early mission forces in Sierra Leone. They can readily be distinguished from the perils which struck down Smith and O'Neill on the way to Uganda. They were but distantly related to the sorrows which fell thick and fast during the early history of the Universities Mission to Eastern Equatorial Africa. They do not suggest comparison with the marvellous story of peril and of triumph associated with Mr. Duncan's early work in Metlakahtla. The Pacific missions abound in many more incidents that touch the popular imagination. The story of Allen Gardiner and of the South American Mission appears far more stirring to the emotional side of our natures. And yet, as it seems to me, the pioneers of Christianity amongst the awakened Japanese worked under conditions so remarkable that they well deserve a place to themselves. They had a past to redeem, and although that past had been made and marred by the pioneers of the Roman Catholic faith, it was the name of Christianity which had thereby come into disrepute so signal.

That name it was for Protestant workers to clear.

The earlier history of Christian missions in Japan was of a kind both to encourage and discourage new attempts. In the steps of Mendez Pinto, whose ship the storms carried to the coast of Japan in 1542, there followed, after an interval of seven years, no less a person than Francis Xavier. A native, who had found his way to Goa, assured Xavier that his countrymen would listen to a missionary's message, compare his life with his teaching, and, if satisfied, flock to Christ. The statement was encouraging, and Xavier lost little time in acting upon it. The field surely was inviting; a calm hearing and a candid examination promised to the preachers of the new faith! In some respects that early statement might be made of the Japanese to-day. They too hear, watch, and compare. But for us there lies a danger less conspicuous in Xavier's time, for all Europeans who profess Christianity must by their conduct witness for or against the faith. They have not always been living evidences of its worth. Sir Rutherford Alcock, writing more than three centuries after the words of Xavier's convert, numbered amongst the obstacles to missionary enterprise in Japan the shocking contrast between the doctrines preached by the missionaries and the manner of life practised by the average European resident.

Xavier reached Japan in August 1549, and he found his way amid many privations, against many difficulties, and with much suffering, to the capital. To himself, however, but little success was granted. Yet he had scarcely left the land, after a sojourn of two or three years, before the new doctrines found acceptance everywhere. Thirty years after Xavier's arrival there were 150,000 converts in Japan. It seemed a mere question of calculation what time should elapse before all the land would be Christian. This success may have been due in part to political causes; yet, remembering subsequent events, we have no reason to estimate lightly the faith of those Jesuit converts. But success brought its own perils. Buddhism was persecuted with all the horrors which Rome of that period so freely used. Rome took the sword, and presently fell thereby. She conspired against the ruling powers, and by them was ruthlessly dealt with.

The Shogûn issued in 1587 a decree of expulsion against the Jesuits, whom he deemed, with good reason, hostile to the independence of Japan. Persecution resulting, civil war ensued. In the East they know how to torture. Neither Chinese nor Japanese had much to learn from the West in that. But the things done in the name of Christianity might to the popular mind have excused the cruelties practised upon its confessors. With such measure as the Jesuits had been wont to mete it was measured to their converts again. How did they bear it? Not the records of the early Christian Church, not the history of that dark era in the Christian life of Madagascar, not the story of the young converts hewn piecemeal to death or roasted alive in Uganda, show nobler faith than that of these Japanese Romanists. The ingenuity of the East spent itself in devising new tortures, but spent itself in vain. The unfaithful were few. Long the terror raged, until at last an unsuccessful blow for freedom left nearly forty thousand Christians at once in the hands of their oppressors. Their reward was death. Yet Christianity was not extinguished. Lacking the Bible, it could not grow as under the same terms it had grown in Madagascar; but it lingered on in corners, and as late as 1829 martyrs were found to suffer. This, in spite of a native inquisition which, from 1636 until the treaties with Christian nations, provided for due inquiry into the faith of suspected persons. A plate graven with a representation of the Saviour had to be trodden upon by suspects who would avoid condemnation. Even as late as 1869 persecution tore from their homes three thousand natives who were of this remnant. And, lest Xavier should have successors from over the sea, the public notice-boards of the Empire displayed an inscription which began thus:

"So long as the sun shall warm the earth, let no Christian be so bold as to come to Japan."

Into the history of the causes which broke down the resultant seclusion we need not enter in detail here. They were external and internal; first, pressure from foreign powers, which gave access to certain ports; then the great revolution of 1868, which abolished the feudal system, restored the power of the Mikado, and opened Japan to Western influences. The political and social habits of centuries were then laid aside, and a new era began.

When the first step—the opening of the treaty ports — was made, five American societies established themselves within the prescribed limits; but it was not until the year of the revolution that the Church Missionary Society found the means and the man to attack Japan. In that year the Rev. George Ensor, a Cambridge graduate, was chosen as the first messenger of English Christianity to the New Empire.

There was legal access to the country, but to preach Christ was still against the law of the land. The foreigner, when he took his walks abroad, was reminded of the fact by the omnipresent notices, "The laws hitherto enforced forbidding Christianity are to be strictly observed." This statement did not come of a stolid conservatism which clung to relics of the past when the very cause of their origin was forgotten. Into such grievous disrepute had the political activities of the Jesuits brought Christianity, that the nation was well content to deem it a most dangerous foe. Its long past history was a blot upon the fair fame of the

c

nation. The man who would compass its restoration must needs be an enemy of the commonwealth. This suspicion had little upon which to feed, for it was usual to regard the foreign faith as extinct. Save to a few experts, whose business it was to know the signs by which any adherent of Christianity might be detected, its nature was unknown. But it was a thing to be held in national abhorrence; and even apart from this, whilst the laws against Christianity were still in force, any investigation of its tenets, or curiosity as to its possible value, might be extremely inconvenient to the inquirer. Was it so very long ago that they crucified at Osaka that old woman and those six men who, in their own imperfect way, worshipped Christ?

There was, too, another feeling. Christianity was the faith of the foreigner. Now, despite the marvellous curiosity, eagerness to learn, and readiness to adopt changes, so conspicuous in the New Japan, there were still everywhere men who distrusted all reform, and especially such as touched their faith. Their hearts went back to the old feudal system, and to the old exclusiveness of their earlier days. They could not accommodate themselves, with the facility of a woman wearing a new dress, to the strange sights and sounds and habits which met them at every turn. But if these had to be endured, was it a matter of necessity to take the Western faith also? From the first, men of this stamp had made themselves obnoxious to the foreigner.

Nor, it must be confessed, was their attitude surprising. The morality of the Europeans in the treaty-ports in the earlier days of intercourse was largely inferior to that of the Japanese themselves. Whilst, therefore, the missionaries preached, the lay European often practised in a way that made his nominal faith a by-word and reproach. Further, the old religions of the land had a large official following. The census of 1875 showed that there were, for a population of about 35,000,000, no fewer than 207,000 priests, monks, nuns, and other "religious" persons. Moreover, both Buddhism and Shintoism had been closely allied with the State; and even before the final severance between Church and State in 1884, the devotees of either faith could have foreseen the inevitable results of contact with Western ideas upon the old religions as well as upon the social life of the country.

We have said enough to show that the attempt upon Japan was by no means a matter of simplicity or one free from peril. Mr. Ensor's destination was Nagasaki, the treaty-port in the island of Kiu-Shiu. It was here, cabined, cribbed, and confined to the limits of the island of Deshima, that the Dutch, for 230 years, had conducted that trade with Japan which was the only link—saving an annual junk from China—between the outside world and the self-contained Land of the Rising Sun. Mr. Ensor's first view of the shore showed him the singular beauty of the country, but reminded him also that Christianity was a perilous thing to profess. For there before him frowned at the entrance of the bay the rock Pappenberg, from whose summit it is generally believed that they hurled many of the Christians crushed in the last rising of 1637. What was possible in a land which had shown the marvellous resolution evidenced, both in nearly three centuries of exclusiveness, and in a war of extermination against the professors of a faith it had learned to distrust?

Scarcely was he settled before he was granted another reminder of the antagonism to Christianity. Past his door were driven hundreds of Romanists, forming nearly the whole population of a village near Nagasaki, who, under the laws against Christianity, were torn from their homes and sent into banishment. The Roman Catholic accounts represent them as suffering the cruellest treatment; and, although the result of Sir Harry Parkes's inquiries would seem to show that there was some exaggeration in these, Mr. Ensor is witness that their condition and experiences excited the strongest commiseration.

There was already one Protestant missionary, representing an American Society, settled in Nagasaki; but his presence, if to some extent reassuring, did not tell Mr. Ensor that the ordinary methods of evangelisation were available. The laws made it impossible to open a small preaching-place, or to collect hearers in the open air, or to invite the children to a school. To sit at home and await inquiries, that, of course, was possible. But would not such a policy be an invitation of the mountain to come to Mohammed? So it might reasonably have seemed; but so in reality it was not. The spirit of inquiry was abroad, and included religion within its scope. It may be that there was, in many instances, no strong spiritual craving at the root of these inquiries. It was the great West of which the keen-witted Japanese wished to talk, and it was impossible for them to ignore her religion either as a matter of interest by itself, or in relation to its influence upon learning, art, and social life.

But the man who ventured to ask about Christianity might be discerned by the greater caution of his approach. It came to Mr. Ensor's ears that the Government had stationed a watch at his gate. The precaution would doubtless be known to the public, and would suggest measures of self-protection to any who wished to know something of that evil sect called Christian.

When from his dwelling Mr. Ensor looked out into the gloom of night, it was at least trying to be uncertain as to the intentions of the figures cautiously approaching his door. They might be emissaries of the Government; they might be fanatics bent on removing a teacher of the long-condemned faith; they might be more of those visitors who—polite, voluble, full of eager curiosity—had hour by hour flocked to him for news of great England across the sea. For long he lay down at night deeming it quite possible that a violent death might be his before morning. But every hour of the day brought its own anxiety, whilst success in the work promised even more peril than failure.

When under the cover of night the cautious inquirer had reached Mr. Ensor's presence, it was well to think of his safety. The doors were closed, the windows barred; then teacher and learner sat in converse till startled by another knock. Was this the summons of friend or of foe? For the most part it was another inquirer, who could only be talked with when the first was gone. When they parted, it was with the parting of men who felt that each had placed his life in the other's hands.

Soon definite encouragement cheered the pioneer. In the very week that Mr. Ensor saw the Urakami Christians being driven into exile, there came to him, under the shadow of night, one who was something more than a mere inquirer. When the knock was answered Mr. Ensor found an armed Japanese at the door. Beckoned in, and asked to explain his wishes, the visitor said: "A few days ago I had a copy of the Bible in my hands, and I wish to be a Christian."

The statement was astonishing. Could the man be bent on some malicious purpose?

"Are you a stranger in these parts?" asked Mr. Ensor. "Don't you know that thousands of the people are being detained as prisoners for this?"

"Yes," said the man, "I know. Last night I came to your gate, and as I stood there, thinking of the danger of the step I was about to take, fear overpowered me and I returned. But there stood by me in the night one who came to me in my dreams, and said I was to go to the house of the missionary, and nothing would happen to me; and I have come."

Then the stranger drew his sword, and on it swore, by a Japanese oath, that he would be true to his teacher.

This man was one of the first of Mr. Ensor's converts. With his baptism began the building of a native church, which may now be said to represent a national rather than an external organisation. That convert was received in the winter of 1870. The statistics of the Japan mission of the Church Missionary Society, as stated in the report for the year 1892-93, show that the adherents numbered 2457, with no fewer than 80 ordained and lay native workers.

The advance has everywhere been steady and hopeful. Indeed, within fifteen years of that baptism thoughtful Japanese had begun to discuss the desirability of making Christianity the national faith. Behind these suggestions there did not, for the most part, lie any personal attachment to the faith, but only a philosophic conviction that Christianity was the religion for a progressive nation. Once upon a time it was even proposed to baptise the Emperor and some of the nobles, as a sign or token that the faith long banished from Japan was now the official faith of the land. They have resisted that temptation, and we cannot doubt the wisdom of their resolve. In spite of a certain strenuous effort to revive the power of the old religions, Christianity is steadily making its way throughout Japan. Even the old aboriginal Ainus have felt its force. It is better that a national Christianity should thus be reached step by step, than that the voice of authority should recommend it to the people. We want and we have toleration; we do not want patronage, that may prove the fruitful parent of formalism and hypocrisy.

THE GRAVES BY THE VICTORIA NYANZA

THE GRAVES BY THE VICTORIA NYANZA

No mission of modern times has won more attention from the outside public than the bold attempt of the Church Missionary Society to rear a native Church by the shores of the Victoria Nyanza. Through circumstances over which the missionaries themselves had no control, their labours acquired a national interest. It is not good for missions when they impinge upon the field of politics. But if that cannot be avoided, it is all the more important that we should have clearly in mind the work of those who, never dreaming of imperial interests casting long shadows across their path, or of politicians debating the conditions of its continuance, have lived and died in simple obedience to their Master's command.

In the attempt on Uganda they have died in

divers ways—under the sudden assault of natives before Europeans were familiar objects; by premeditated murder; by fever, even before they had reached their goal, and before the sound of home farewells had quite died out of their ears; by fever, after enduring many sorrows, and passing unscathed through many perils. The death-roll of the Uganda mission, counting those who died on their way up from the coast, and one whose enfeebled frame the heat of the Red Sea exhausted, marks it as a mission of peculiar peril. Perhaps that is why recruits have never been wanting.

The native Church in Uganda is one product of what, for the time, seemed a blow at missionary enterprise. When, in 1843, John Ludwig Krapf, expelled from Abyssinia, was also expelled from Shoa, a man of less faith and pertinacity might have argued that Africa was closed against him. Not so with him. Repelled there, he only sought for another opening into the same continent. He sailed from Aden in an Arab dhow, and in January 1844 landed at Mombasa. It was he who first heard of the great inland sea. It was from his companions, Rebmann and Erhardt, that the sketch-map of the great lake, which set all the geographical quidnuncs of Europe a-talking, came. It was from this that resulted the expedition of Burton and Speke, of Speke and Grant, the later explorations of Livingstone, and the journeys which brought Mr. Stanley to Uganda. It was from Mr. Stanley's interview with Mtesa that sprang Mtesa's appeal, through Mr. Stanley, for missionary teachers, in answer to which the Church Missionary Society's Nyanza mission was organised. Thus the expulsion from Abyssinia and Shoa, so far from throwing back the progress of the Gospel, resulted in the standard of the Cross being raised in the very centre of Equatorial Africa.

It was on November 15, 1875, that readers of the *Daily Telegraph* found in its pages a letter from Mr. Stanley, conveying Mtesa's invitation for missionaries. By June 26, 1876, the members of the first expedition, prepared by the Church Missionary Society in answer to that call, were at Zanzibar.

They were a remarkable band. The leader

was Lieutenant Shergold Smith. His father was, as a midshipman, on board the man-of-war by which Crowther, afterwards Bishop of the Niger Territory, was saved from the slave-ship in 1822. He himself had served with distinction in the Ashanti war, but had retired from the Army in order to enter the ministry. He was the first volunteer. Alexander Mackay, the young Scotch engineer, a man of Livingstone's mould, was the second. Dr. John Smith, a friend from Edinburgh, joined at his request. A Manchester curate, the Rev. C. T. Wilson, offered; so did Mr. T. O'Neill, an architect; Mr. James Robertson, a builder, from Newcastle; Mr. G. J. Clarke, an engineer; and Mr. W. M. Robertson, an artisan. The Society's doctors rejected Mr. James Robertson, wherefore he went out with the party at his own charges.

When the Committee bade them farewell, Mackay, the youngest of all, offered a word of warning, the gist of which may be given in one of its sentences: "I want to remind the Committee that within six months they will probably hear that one of us is dead."

That was in April 1876. The forecast was

justified. On August 5, the man whom no doctors could keep from the field, Mr. James Robertson, died at Zanzibar. But although the two artisans broke down, and were sent home, and although Mackay was for a time invalided, the remnant struggled on. In January 1877, Wilson and O'Neill reached the south end of the Victoria Nyanza, the borders, as it were, of the land they sought. And there Dr. John Smith died in May. In December of that year, Shergold Smith and O'Neill were murdered by a native chief, to whose vengeance they refused to surrender an Arab trader who sought their protection. Thus, of the original band, Shergold Smith, O'Neill, Dr. John Smith, and James Robertson were dead; W. Robertson and G. J. Clark had been invalided home; Wilson and Mackay alone remained. The former was with Mtesa, in Uganda, the latter toiling up from the coast. The first steps had been costly; it needed men of faith and patience to go on.

But recruits were coming. And of them also death at once took toll. Two artisans for Uganda had landed at Zanzibar in June 1877, but one almost immediately broke down, and was sent home; the other died on the journey to the Lake. It was not until July 1878, that Mackay reached the south end of the Victoria Nyanza. Wilson crossed from Mtesa's to meet him, and the two were wrecked on their way back.

But other recruits were coming. Five, helped by General Gordon, were travelling up the Nile; the others were journeying by Zanzibar. Of this latter party, one, Mr. Penrose, was murdered by robbers; and one from each party had been invalided home. Early in 1879 there were, for a time, seven Church Missionary Society missionaries in Uganda, but two came home with Mtesa's envoys to the Queen, and two were sent to Uyui, a station south of the Lake.

For a little while Mtesa was friendly, and teaching possible. Then came more misfortunes. Mr. Litchfield's health compelled his departure, and Mackay saw him part of the way home. Mr. Pearson, left alone in Uganda, was nearly starved to death. He might have died, in the midst of plenty, but for gifts from some of the natives. Hardest of all, teaching was forbidden, and a lad, who persisted that the religion of Jesus was the only true religion, was put into the stocks, and afterwards deported from the capital. The solitary young worker, his life at the mercy of a fickle savage, forbidden to tell his message, getting protection by putting up a flagstaff for the king, fed by the gifts of people he had doctored, and uncheered by ease of communication with home, needed faith and patience in no common degree. He had both; for amidst it all his request for himself is " Lord, clear the way . . . . enable us to light Thy candle in Uganda, which shall never be put out."

Then, for a while, there were better times. Teaching was allowed, hearers flocked in, converts were baptized, and Mackay (who had arrived) was, with a toy printing-press, trying to satisfy the demand for literature. By the end of 1884 there had been eighty-eight baptisms; and the mission staff was again strengthened, for another party of six had left England in May 1882. Of those six, Hannington was murdered three years later, under circumstances presently to be described; Blackburn lies in God's acre at Usambiro, at the south end of the Lake.

In 1884 Mtesa died. His successor, Mwanga, a lad of eighteen, was readily persuaded to oppose the white men and their teaching. The next crisis in the history of the mission is soon, therefore, reached. In January 1885, Mackay and Ashe, travelling with two native boys, were stopped by a Mohammedan chief, and marched back, under guard, to the capital. Inquiry as to the fate of the boys only brought down further violence. Presents failed to appease the authorities, and soon the two missionaries found their worst fears confirmed; for the two lads and another young Christian had been burnt to death.

"Our hearts are breaking," wrote Mackay. "All our Christians dispersed"—they had bidden them to seek safety in flight—"we are lonely and deserted, sad and sick." But in a day or two he is full of hope once more, resolved that if the missionaries are driven out, they shall leave Christian literature behind them. In the same spirit, when Mwanga protested that the boys had been martyred without his knowledge, Mackay boldly told the tyrant that he had "committed a great sin against God in murdering innocent boys." It was a crisis to try the stoutest heart. Death might come at any moment; and at the time of gravest peril the mission boat was swamped. Little wonder that the prolonged strain laid O'Flaherty aside with fever.

That crisis passed. There came a little season of prosperity again, when Mackay could freely admonish the king. But even whilst he thus leant one ear to instruction, Mwanga gave his head executioner liberty to slay as he pleased. It was obvious that the infant Church was but enjoying a respite. Sooner or later the blow would fall, and who would survive it? It fell first, not upon the party in Uganda, but upon one coming, as Mackay hoped, to its succour.

James Hannington, driven back to England in 1883, had resolved to return in the following year. It was decided that he should go out as first Bishop of Eastern Equatorial Africa. He was consecrated, and reached his diocese in 1884. In the following year he started for Uganda. Along the old route, to the south end of the Lake, the missionary parties had suffered so severely from the exactions of tribute-asking chiefs, that Hannington resolved to strike out a new line, through Masailand, to the north end of the Lake. The peril from the then all-powerful Masai was deemed so great that every effort was used to move Hannington from his resolve; but he believed the need of a new road to be so urgent that he resolved to face the perils. Through the perils predicted he passed in safety; danger and death came from an unlooked-for quarter.

Mwanga lay in dread of Europeans seeking to "eat up" his country. When some of his raiders brought news from Busoga that "there were two white men there, and some more behind with a great caravan," he seems to have felt that the flood was pouring in. To the three watchers in Uganda there was presently borne word that the stranger was, as they feared, their Bishop, and that he was already in the stocks. Then followed long hours of agony as they waited for news.

At last it came. Hannington was dead. To us now his own journals tell almost of all save the very last scene. He was led to execution, singing, after the pattern of many other martyrs, hymns in which men caught the name of Jesus. The story of his life and death has been told by a friend, and has inspired a work by a master-hand in fiction. His example has borne much fruit, and may bear still more for the profit of Africa.

Hannington was slain on October 29, 1885. It is characteristic of the mission, and the men who worked it, that on this day Mackay and Ashe, having sent their native helpers into hiding, spent the time, one in revising his translation of St. Matthew, the other in putting it into type. If they were to die they would at least leave the witness behind them. Within a week of Hannington's death there were five more baptisms. Inquirers pressed in; whilst Mwanga swung from praise to anger, from applause to threats of death, from fears of the missionary's power to the burning of the converts.

The storm soon burst. On May 25, 1886, an order went forth for the arrest of all the Christians. At least eleven converts were killed that day; shortly afterwards thirty-two were burnt alive, "calling on God." Yet even so, the Church prospered, and inquirers grew bolder. The impotence of persecution struck even the native chiefs, and the king's proposal to kill Mackay met with no countenance. But to have lived through those months of agony was surely to have compressed the sorrows of a lifetime. In August 1886, Mr. Ashe at last obtained leave to quit Uganda, and the heroic Mackay was for a while left to face the situation alone.

There was no lack of work for him to do, for still, as evening fell, the people came. "Late, late, often very late, we wound up, and I was often more than exhausted—reading, teaching, drudging, etc."—one man a light to a nation. And this amidst alarms and threats, when again there were deaths and escapes from death. Amongst the escapes was that of Mika Sematimba, then an officer in the king's bodyguard, who, at the end of 1892, came to England with the Rev. R. H. Walker. Opposition increased once more. Mohammedan slavers diligently worked to secure the death or expulsion of Mackay; and even the French missionaries seem to have welcomed the prospect of his dismissal. It was hard to leave; but at last he judged it best "to bend before the storm." In August, 1887, he reached the south end of the Lake, and ultimately fixed his home at Usambiro.

Yet Uganda was left but for a very little while without an English occupant. Mackay's place was almost at once taken by the Rev. E. C. Gordon, a nephew of the murdered Hannington, a recruit from a quiet clerical home in Yorkshire, by the shores of the North Sea. And other helpers might be hoped for, since the new bishop, Henry Perrott Parker, with Mr. Ashe and others, would shortly reach Usambiro. They came, and one of the party, the Rev. R. H. Walker, went on to Uganda.

But death was again to be busy with the mission. On the very day, in May 1888, when the Church Missionary Society was keeping its anniversary at Exeter Hall, came news that the bishop and Mr. Blackburn were both dead. Fever took them both, and they were buried at Usambiro. The loss of Bishop Parker was a heavy one to the mission. Already it had had two bishops, and neither of them had survived the attempt to reach Uganda. Yet lest the men should be overmuch cast down at this new discipline, great encouragement came to the mission. Mwanga watched in vain for some of the Christian natives whom he sought to kill. Two of them ventured out of hiding and boldly helped in the work of teaching, but had once more to flee. Mr. Gordon, the solitary watcher in Uganda, was strengthened by the arrival, in

April 1888, of the Rev. R. H. Walker. Before these two there lay trials only less severe than those which fell on Mackay and Ashe.

Mwanga devised an ingenious plan for exterminating the "readers" by starving them to death on an island. They suspected his motive just in time, and his plot hastened their decision to rise against him. Quietly and without loss of life he was deposed, and left the country. For a while all went well. Then the Mohammedans planned another rising, and for a time succeeded. Messrs. Walker and Gordon, with the French missionaries, were at their mercy. Happily, though they robbed them with cruel completeness, they stopped short of murder. With little or no provision the white men were put on board the Church Missionary Society's boat and left to the tender mercies of the great lake. A hippopotamus capsized the boat, but happily near the land. Five native boys were drowned; but the white men escaped, and Mr. Walker patched up the leak as best he could. "I confess," he says, "I felt bad as we rowed away from shore, miles away from land, thirty-four souls on board, and only a pad of tow and dripping to keep the water out." Seventeen days of such an experience were enough to try the stoutest heart. And not so many months before Mr. Walker had been curate of All Souls', Langham Place—a sufficiently striking contrast.

After a while another revolution placed the Christians again in power, and back with them went the young pair, Gordon and Walker. Upon the Christian subjects whom he had so long persecuted Mwanga had now to rely, and for a time he was fully sensible of their use to him. It was during the perils which succeeded his return to power that Mwanga and the Christian party sought help from the representatives of the British East Africa Company. In these and subsequent negotiations the missionaries shared, but only as interpreters or agents, and not as leaders or persons of authority.

Only two scenes in the chequered recent history of the mission need here be noticed. In February 1890, the heroic Mackay died of fever at Usambiro, and was laid in the little graveyard, near his bishop. He had refused to come home, but sent instead repeated calls for reinforcements. Mackay's career touched the public imagination more than that of any missionary since the death of Livingstone. His patience, his faith, his many-sided usefulness, all appealed to a wider circle than those immediately concerned in missionary enterprise.

In April 1890, Bishop Tucker was consecrated, and two bands of recruits went at once out to the field. The history of the second little band is worthy of notice. The group preceding it lost one member almost as soon as it reached the coast. A telegram then asked for further help. It came on May 5th, as the Society was beginning its anniversary, and the contents were made known. The volunteers must be ready to start at once. By ten the next morning, four offered; by the next evening, five more; and on May 10th the chosen four sailed. Of these four one died in two months, one in the November of that year, and one in April 1892.

Yet recruits have not been wanting to fill these places. Is there not heroism in the faith and the patience of the men who have so calmly persevered—

> "Each stepping where his comrade stood
> The instant that he fell"?

A PIONEER IN THE FAR WEST

A PIONEER IN THE FAR WEST

In 1845 a boy named John Horden was elected to the school of St. John's Hospital, Exeter. Into his hands one day there fell a book which described in graphic terms the horrors of heathendom in India. That book decided the character of the boy's life. From the day he read it his desire was to be a missionary. Now in the thirties and forties (and even much later) the missionary calling was viewed in a very different way from what it is now. The Christian Church was far from enthusiastic in its support of missions; the general public viewed them with ill-concealed contempt; the secular press roundly condemned and derided both the work and the workers. Little surprise need therefore be felt at John Horden's wish finding no favour with his friends.

But opposition is not always a bad thing. In

the case of John Horden it conduced in a very striking way to his ultimate success in the mission-field. For on leaving school he learned a trade, and that was one advantage in the years to come. Then he became a schoolmaster, and in struggling with the problems that beset every thoughtful teacher, he gained another store of experience for the great work of his life. Nor was he ever forgetful of the mission-field. At Exeter he was for some years one of a band of young men who met regularly to read the Bible and keep themselves informed of missionary work. Of that company two became missionaries of the Society for the Propagation of the Gospel, and four of the Church Missionary Society.

In his twenty-third year the old longing for work in the mission-field came upon Horden with overwhelming force. This time he was able to take the definite step of offering himself to the Church Missionary Society, and by it he was in the latter part of 1850 accepted for training. If the schoolboy aspirations of young John Horden had been at once recognised by his friends he could hardly have been sent out at an earlier age;

nor could his prior training have been of a more useful character.

It was to India that Horden's thoughts had turned as a boy, and on India his hopes were fixed when he offered himself to the Church Missionary Society. To India, also, he would probably have gone but for another of those interpositions which are so prominent in his life.

In May 1851, when the minds of people at home were occupied with thoughts of the Great Exhibition in Hyde Park, there came to the Church Missionary Society House news that the Wesleyans were about to withdraw from a missionary post they had held at Moose Factory, in the Hudson's Bay Territory. It was in the highest degree important, in the opinion of those who knew the Indians and their needs, that this post should not be given up, and the Church Missionary Society Committee lent a willing ear to the appeal. But who could go out? Horden's offer and his qualifications were remembered; he was telegraphed for, and the Committee's need laid before him. He had thought of India; this pointed to America. He had dreamed of crowded cities and thronging thousands amongst whom to do the work of an evangelist; he was shown a few Indians whose surroundings suggested neither romance nor excitement.

But Horden's wish to be a missionary was no sentimental affection born of picturesque description or touching appeal. He meant work, and he was willing to be guided. Without hesitation he accepted the Committee's suggestion. They asked when he could be ready; his answer was, "Within a week." This was late in May. There was no time to be lost, for only one ship a year went to the Bay, and it was desirable that the missionary should sail at once. So great, too, was the isolation, that he was advised to take a wife with him. Horden had no impediment to allege. He was engaged to a young lady like-minded with himself, and he went down to Devonshire to be married at once. Two days later the young people came up to London, and on June 1st they sailed in the annual ship for Moose. Early in May, Horden had been plodding quietly along at his work in Devonshire; at the end of August he was a married missionary with a congregation on the shores of Hudson's Bay.

A glance at the map of North America shows

us a southern prolongation of Hudson's Bay, to which the name of James Bay is given. At its extreme south, and a few miles up a river, lies Moose Fort or Moose Factory. It owes its existence to the Hudson's Bay Company, whose officers and servants form a small European population. From a missionary point of view the advantage of Moose consisted not merely in its being the headquarters of the Company's operations, and so enjoying some means of communication—though at very rare intervals—with the outside world, but in its commanding, as it were, the vast desolate regions lying along the eastern and western shores of the Bay.

The people amongst whom John Horden was to become a power belonged to more than one race. In the north, on either side of the bay, were the Esquimaux, the first of the natives to be met on his voyage. The Chipwyans were neighbours of the Esquimaux on the western side. To the south of these on the one side were the Esquimaux, on the other were the Crees. The rest of the interior the Ojibbeways filled.

It was a vast parish, and although at first Horden's labours were local, they extended until, as bishop, he overlooked and directed mission-stations on both shores of the bay, from Fort Churchill on the one side to Little Whale River on the other. On the map the vastness of the distances to be traversed does not strike us, although a diocese 1,500 miles from north to south and east to west, a diocese with some 3,000 miles of rocky coast, is ample enough. But let the conditions of travel be thoroughly understood.

To reach Moose by ship is a perilous voyage, in which the struggle with shoals, rocks, and icebergs has to be conducted with the utmost caution during the few short months that navigation is possible at all. Upon land there are no roads, but in summer the interior is traversed on its waterways by long and perilous voyages in the birch-bark canoe. In the winter, from October to May, the dog-drawn carriole or the snow-shoe is the only means available. From England news and stores came once a year; with other parts of the mission-field there was also some communication. But so great are the difficulties that, when the outgoing ship was one year detained by ice in the bay, the news reached

England before it was known at Albany, a hundred miles from Moose.

Such were the conditions of life into which the young Devonshire schoolmaster was suddenly thrown. "This is, indeed, a day of hope, a day of great thanksgiving," he wrote in his diary on landing; and, in this hopeful, buoyant spirit, which marked all his life, he at once began work.

There were two very obvious advantages: the presence and sympathy of a few Europeans, and the existence of a Christian congregation. The Indians were only too thankful that a missionary was with them once more. Horden at once applied himself to the study of the language, and his remarkable success was due not less to his industry than to his ingenuity of method. He believed in the advantages possessed by a "house-going parson," and was much in the Indians' tents. There he laboriously copied out the conversations he heard, obtained translations, and carefully puzzled out the relation of the two. His success was so rapid that when he had been a year in the work he was an accomplished linguist, able not only to talk with the people, but also to conduct services and preach in the vernacular. Almost on landing he aspired after a printing-press, by which he could give the people reading matter; and he soon began that translational work which will, in the Hudson's Bay Territory, be a lasting memorial of John Horden.

In 1852, the summer after Horden's landing, there came a visitor to Moose. It was the Bishop of Rupertsland, who had journeyed 1,500 miles to visit this outlying station of the then undivided diocese. His original plan had been to establish at Moose a young clergyman whose arrival was expected, and to take Horden back to the Red River, where his preparation for holy orders might go on under the Bishop's eye. But instead of a raw young missionary still struggling with the first difficulties of new and solitary work, he found one already an expert. Horden had won the hearts of the Indians. In the midst of answering the Bishop's questions as to their souls' health, they would break off to ask anxiously if Mr. Horden was to leave them. "He has their hearts and affections," the Bishop wrote in his diary. Moreover, the young schoolmaster had shown extraordinary aptitude for language. "I looked over Mr. Horden's books in the syllabic character, and was astonished at what he had accomplished in so short a time." The Crees used a language which Horden could speak and his Bishop could not. The young people were learned in a kind of Shorter Catechism which Horden had written in their own tongue. He had shown no less conspicuous readiness in adapting himself to the new conditions of life. Clearly he was the man for that mission. The Bishop saw his way through the difficulty. He examined Horden, ordained him deacon and priest in the little church at Moose, and arranged that the clergyman at first destined for that station should take up another. To the last, Moose, his first home in the field, remained Horden's headquarters.

The hardships of life in the Far West were early impressed on the young missionary. In 1854 he had to battle with starvation amongst his flock—a contest repeated again and again. Some, he learned, were driven to cannibalism, and it was one of the greatest joys of his life to see a notable offender, weaned from heathenism, become a patient, consistent Christian. But success was early given, and after only eleven years of work, he estimated that 1,800 Indians in his district were either baptized or waiting for baptism.

I do not propose to tell in detail the story of Horden's work. He was consecrated first Bishop of Moosonee in 1872; he died suddenly in January 1893, amongst his own people. He went as the one missionary on all the shores of the great bay; he left it dotted with mission-stations. He began with a few Christian Indians; he lived to see heathenism renounced by almost all, and many of the Esquimaux also reached.

But despite Selwyn and Patteson, and Hannington and Valpy French, a bishop is sometimes deemed to have an easy life. Let us see how Horden fared. No one ever said less of his own hardships than he; yet they were stern enough. In common with the Europeans and natives, the missionary was largely dependent for food and clothing and the few simple comforts of life in the Far West upon the arrival of the annual ship. Every year the anxiety was great as its time drew near, and equally great the joy on the ship's appearance. Every year, too, much depended on the coming of the geese, for, salted down, they supplied food for many months. Want and starvation were familiar in most winters; epidemics scarcely less common.

Horden's letters show us a many-sided life. Now he is meeting the Indians as they bring in their furs, hearing of their sorrows and joys since last they met, reproving, rebuking, exhorting. Anon he is by the bedside of a dying Christian, hearing such words of faith, and peace, and thankfulness, as repay a life of toil. Presently he is planning a tour of 1,500 or 2,000 miles, when "his lordship" will sleep a good deal in the open, and fare as the Indians do. Then he is nursing the sick and restoring hope in the face of an epidemic which has taken courage as well as strength from all. Again, he is going steadily over his translation of the Bible, that he may leave it as perfect as possible before he is called away. He is a bishop, but he can "knit as well as any old woman," manage a birch-bark canoe, turn the legs for a table, help the smith at the forge, cook his own dinner, compose the hymns for an ordination service, put them into type, and print them for his people. Of complaint—save that he cannot get all the help he wants for the mission—there is none; of thankfulness and contentment much.

Writing less than twelve months before his death, he said: "As far as postal communication is concerned, we do not, as the years roll on, get any nearer to the outside world; we are still buried in the interminable forest, the door of our grave being opened but seldom. We should like it to be different, but we know it is no good repining. Like almost everything else, this has its bright as well as its dark side; we have no distractions, our work goes on continuously, our minds become fully absorbed by our surroundings, and I doubt there being many happier communities than the one to be found where the hand of God has placed me; the wheels of our little society move smoothly, and, with God in our midst, we envy none the advantages they possess, and are contented with our own diminutive world."

Writing home in June 1884, the Bishop gave a picturesque account of a five-days' journey inland to a station, Long Portage House, up the Moose River. Though in the month of June, the weather was cold; there was rain and snow, and a long canoe voyage was no child's play.

"Painfully poling or tracking-up" the canoe in the various rapids, or paddling between banks heaped to thirty feet high with blocks of ice, camping out at night, "his lordship" sped on, that at the end of the journey he might minister at the most to a handful of people. They gathered, when he came, in the trader's sitting-room, and then, when the baptisms, the confirmations, and the other services were over, the Bishop set off once more for Moose. In the five days' journeying out they had met but one family; on the way back they came upon a body of Indians. There was a halt at once; a service of three hours' duration was begun upon the spot; and then the Bishop's little band went into camp at 10.30 P.M., to be up and in the canoes again at four.

In September of the same year he describes a lake journey upon a similar mission. This time, as the crews camped upon the shore the tents were twice flooded by the rising tide. At the end of that journey he had to comfort a little flock which had lost entire families by starvation in the preceding winter, and had then been attacked by influenza. Scarcely had he returned from this journey when a cry of distress reached him from another station a hundred miles away. "I went at once," he says in his own simple fashion. It meant another toilsome canoe journey through bad weather, even for Moosonee.

At the station he found influenza raging in such wise that it threatened to sweep away the whole population. But the presence of this one strong man gave all new hope; the sick revived; and after nearly five weeks of nursing, cheering, and teaching, Horden could turn his face again homeward, "leaving no one seriously ill." The mosquitoes were a trouble on that journey; but in the following letter he has to tell the story of a ship's crew frozen up in the bay, with the thermometer at 48° below zero. The extremes of temperature to which the country is subject were trying to the European. In summer the thermometer might be 100° in the shade, in the winter 50° below zero.

Whatever trials befell the Mission or the Indians under his care, Horden never lost heart or good-humour. Here is his own account of one incident which admirably illustrates his contentment under hardship. He is on one of his long canoe journeys. "We put ashore on a rocky point for breakfast; we lit our fire and put on our kettles, but before they had time to boil a most terrific storm broke out, which at once extinguished our fire; the rain, accompanied by a fall of large hailstones, many of them as large as pistol bullets, some as large as musket balls, was tremendous, while the thunder and lightning were deafening and blinding. The violence of the storm apparently soon spent itself, and we lit the fire a second time, being now allowed to complete the cooking. Myself and the archdeacon sat down to breakfast encased in our waterproofs, breakfast being composed of bread, coffee, and dried goose, the latter very good, but very, very hard. We had scarcely sat two minutes when the storm broke out again with redoubled violence; but it was not to again deprive me of my breakfast, of which I felt very much in need, so I simply placed my bread under my plate and sat it out. The rain did for milk in my hot coffee, and somewhat softened my hard goose; if it made it a little insipid it did not much matter to an old traveller like myself; of the bread I took a pinch as I required it; then as if to reward us for our constancy, the storm after a while ceased and allowed us to finish our meal in peace."

On yet another journey the Bishop is drawn by a team of dogs, which do forty miles in a little over six hours. When night came the little party looked for rest and then another early start.

"But this was not to be; the weather was very rough, and the atmosphere so thick that nothing seaward was visible, so we remained in camp and passed most of the day in reading. I had placed the *Sunday Magazine* in my hand-bag, and this proved a source of much interest to us all."

Writing in February 1885, the Bishop has to record "the formal opening of the chancel of our cathedral." Of course, it was a building of the simplest kind, but its furniture and decorations were at least remarkable in one respect, since they were largely made by Horden himself. It is not every cathedral that displays the handi-work of its Bishop.

As nearly all the Indians in the diocese of Moosonee have now become Christians, we shall be quite prepared to hear them denounced in some quarters as persons of little independence or resolution. A single fact may usefully be introduced here. In 1886 the Bishop records the death of a native Christian, "only an Indian," but one whose story "might well read a good lesson to many a more highly civilised member of human society."

Eliza married a hunter. There came a hard winter; two of the children died of starvation; she and her husband grew more and more exhausted. It was seventy miles to the nearest point at which aid could be obtained. But Eliza tied her two surviving little ones on a sledge, and, preceded by her husband, set off to that point. Soon the husband's strength gave out. Then Eliza lit a fire, extemporised a shelter, placed her husband within it, and drawing the sledge behind her, pushed on for Albany. Her strength held out till she reached it, then she fell unconscious. When she revived, help was at once sent off to the husband, but they only found a frozen corpse. The children survived, and like their heroic mother grew up devout, consistent Christians.

The story of Horden's last days is partly told in

an unfinished letter from himself, dated January 5, 1893. The Bishop had long suffered acutely from rheumatism, the result of exposure upon his journeys; but one day in the previous November, whilst engaged early in the morning in revising his translations, he was seized with a more serious attack. He revived so far as to have a native helper into his sick-room, with whom he continued to work. But the heart was affected, and on January 12, just a week after he began the letter, he passed quietly away. He now sleeps in the midst of the flock to whom he had given nearly forty-two years of labour.

Horden was of late only one of a small but noble band of Christian bishops working in the vast solitudes that lie between the Canadian Pacific Railway and the Polar seas. Of a truth these are apostles. Each might write himself down as "in journeyings often, in perils of waters . . . in perils in the wilderness . . . in weariness and painfulness, in watchings often, in hunger and thirst, in fastings often, in cold and nakedness. Besides those things that are without, that which cometh upon me daily, the care of all the churches."

THE PILGRIM MISSIONARY OF
THE PUNJAB

THE PILGRIM MISSIONARY OF THE PUNJAB

IN the year 1880 the British forces in Afghanistan sustained a most severe and bloody defeat at the battle of Maiwand. The shattered remnant found refuge in Kandahar, and were there closely besieged, until the brilliant victory gained by Sir Frederick Roberts, after the great march from Kabul to Kandahar, once more set them free.

During the siege a sortie was ordered against a village from which a destructive fire was being poured in upon Kandahar. In the hospital within the walls, helping to receive the wounded as they arrived from the front, was a missionary. After a time he went to the Kabul gate for the same purpose. There they told him of certain wounded men lying untended in a shrine some two or three hundred yards outside. With a dooly and bearers he at once went off to their aid, though the fire was heavy. Arrived at the shrine originally pointed out, he found it empty: the wounded were not there, but at another shrine some thirty yards away. The danger increased at every step, and an officer advised the missionary not to proceed. He could not, however, be persuaded to return; and, whilst starting for the second shrine, he was struck by a bullet. He was taken into Kandahar in the dooly he had brought out for others, and on the same afternoon he died. The missionary who thus fell was George Maxwell Gordon, an honorary agent of the Church Missionary Society.

The "pilgrim missionary of the Punjab" belonged to the band of noble men who, possessing ample means, have dedicated all without reserve to the service of Christ in foreign lands. George Maxwell Gordon might have lived a life of ease at home; he was content to "endure hardness as a good soldier of Jesus Christ." He might have filled posts of honour under less exacting circumstances; he preferred the perils of a pioneer's work in India.

The life of George Maxwell Gordon before he went out to the mission-field is soon told. The son of Captain J. E. Gordon, M.P. for Dundalk, he was born on August 10th, 1839. His father, a man of unbounded energy, and of equal zeal in the cause of Protestantism, was a familiar figure at Exeter Hall in the days of its power. The son was educated at home, and then under the care of the Rev. Henry Moule. In Mr. Moule's vicarage at Fordington, he breathed a missionary atmosphere. Two missionaries went forth from that family; and another son, the Rev. H. C. G. Moule, Principal of Ridley Hall, has done more than any other man living to foster the missionary spirit among the graduates and undergraduates at Cambridge. At eighteen, Gordon entered Trinity, Cambridge, where he graduated in 1861. His own wishes as to a career had been varied. He thought of many paths, but of none of them for long. Once he had wished to be a soldier, then a sailor, then an Indian civilian; "anything, in short, but a clergyman." To the influence of Dr. Marsh and his daughter he owed the readiness to be ordained. It was whilst with Dr. Marsh at Beddington that Gordon met the Rev. Thomas Valpy French, afterwards the heroic Bishop of Lahore. To companionship with French can, no doubt, be traced the genesis of a new aim in life, and to him Gordon first spoke of a desire to be a missionary.

A definite resolution was presently formed, and in 1866 Gordon offered himself to the Church Missionary Society. His wish was to serve without stipend or allowance, and the offer was accepted. Gordon went out to India in the December of that year, and joined the Madras itinerancy. It was the kind of work which exactly suited his athletic frame and his eager temperament, the kind of work to which he always gave himself with delight until his life's end. Yet before long, continuous fever broke down his health, and he went to Australia to recruit. One result of this was a pressing appeal later on, that Gordon should become the first bishop of the new see of Rockhampton, an appeal which he ultimately rejected, to enter upon the work in North India, which led to his death. Returning, he visited Travancore, where the romance of mission life finds the amplest illustration.

His heart went out, however, towards the man and the scenes which had first stirred in him an interest in foreign missions. He came home for a short time in 1870, and the Committee of the Society accepted an offer from Gordon that he should join Mr. French at Lahore. But Gordon was nothing if not thorough. He felt that a knowledge of Persian would be invaluable in the new field, and accordingly resolved to take Persia on the way out, in order to learn the language under the most favourable conditions. In 1871, therefore, we find him in Persia, just when the country was in the throes of famine.

With characteristic zeal he could not use his money to procure ease. "The ride to Teheran," he wrote, "is four hundred miles, and by changing horses every fifteen or twenty miles, and riding day and night, I got to Teheran in five days." The sights by the way and wherever the missionaries went were heart-rending. It was little they could do in their labours "as well for the body as the soul," but Gordon soon found himself acting as "relieving officer, doctor, purveyor, poorhouse guardian and inspector, outfitter, and undertaker to a community of eight hundred poor Armenians." At Shiraz he lodged in one little room, he believed in the same house as that in which Henry Martyn had been. At Hamadan he distributed not only the resources sent from Christians, but also money which Sir Moses Montefiore had remitted for the Jews of that place. The purpose for which he visited Persia was not forgotten, but he saw that work of another kind had been put into his hand.

At the age of thirty-three Gordon found himself with French at Lahore, and teaching in the Divinity School. But his love of evangelistic work drove him to use the college vacation in itinerating. His own ideas entirely coincided with those of French. They both felt the necessity of laying aside as far as possible the signs of the "English gentleman" and approaching the natives much as their own religious enthusiasts would. As he gained experience he began to take some of the students with him upon these tours, until at last itinerating became his only work. Gradually, too, he laid aside one little comfort after another, until he became a veritable fakir.

In time Gordon's plans took the form of a systematic itineracy in a district lying between the Indus and the Jhilam. Working in a methodical way, and inspiring native agents with something of his own enthusiasm, he prepared the whole of his district for the labours of a permanent mission. Then he went farther afield.

Reynell Taylor, one of those Christian soldiers to whose example in India the nation owes so much, had some years before urged the Church Missionary Society to undertake a mission in Derajat. Thither, at the end of 1876, Gordon went. The Bilochis seem at once to have won his heart, and with characteristic generosity the man who lived like a fakir offered 10,000 rupees to start a medical mission amongst them. His inspection over, he returned to other fields.

Later on he was at Delhi, doing the work of an evangelist amongst the native retainers attending princes at the great Durbar, when the Queen was proclaimed Empress of India. Then he was back again in the Jhilam district.

There were yet other fields over which Gordon yearned. In 1878 war broke out with Afghanistan. To Gordon it seemed that this might be a means of carrying the Gospel into a land in which its proclamation was attended with peculiar difficulty and peril. He accordingly offered his services as honorary chaplain for the campaign, and was attached to General Biddulph's command. Gordon's discharge of his new duties was far from formal, as his diaries show. "A very hearty little prayer-meeting in my tent, attended by four officers and eight soldiers," and many like entries witness to the thoroughness of his chaplain life. He returned to his old work to find new helpers. Hurrying on in advance of the returning troops, he surprised his colleagues at Clarkabad. He arrived on foot, accompanied by his spaniel, and looking to the eye of the new-comers very much like an Old Testament prophet. In 1880 he went again to Kandahar, where he fell in the field under the circumstances already described.

Such, in outline, was the missionary life of George Maxwell Gordon. He would have been the last person in the world to write himself down as a hero. He never courted praise, nor sought hardships to win the name of an ascetic. His use of wealth was entirely in the interest of others. He took nothing from the Society with which he worked; he gave it much. The people about him profited more by his purse than he did himself. But he spent his money, and accepted hardships with a purpose —to get at the people.

Thus, itinerating in the Jhilam district, he dispensed with a tent and used the village guest-house, the hospitality of which was shared with the cattle. In larger towns he often followed the same rule, and would shelter in a native inn with the humblest of travellers, in preference to lodging with European friends. On his itinerating tours he did not even care to use the native bedstead as a resting-place; "the ground is good enough," he would say, and upon a little straw or date-palm leaves he slept soundly. In the matter of food he was equally independent; he drank water or milk and water, rarely ate meat, but was content with "chuppaties," fruits and vegetables.

Yet the man who sought no comfort for himself was full of consideration for others. He was known to tramp all day long under the burning sun whilst a weak and sickly native rode his pony. In the cold of the trans-frontier winter he was met one day, miles from his station, without overcoat or vest; he had taken them off to clothe a sick native and child whom he had met by the way suffering from the cold.

Nor was Gordon less mindful of his colleagues. When one of them, itinerating with him upon the frontier, making long marches every day, sheltering at night in the dirty, windowless guest-house of each successive town or village, broke down under the strain, he found in Gordon a nurse tender as a woman. To comfort another, he started at once upon a journey which, in its results, proved to be much even for Gordon's iron constitution. He had five rivers, two of them bridgeless, to cross. One of them, the Indus, was at that season swollen by the melting snows of the Himalayas, and was several miles wide. Beyond its turbid stream, he took horse and rode all night until the Chenab was reached. This crossed by ferry, he arrived at Multan; he took train by night and travelled 200 miles to Lahore; then also by train another hundred miles to Jhilam; and then by boat 50 miles to Pind. All this to comfort a friend. The incident is told in Gordon's own words in the supplementary chapter to Mr. Lewis's account of Gordon's life and work.

On the march into Afghanistan he was equally independent, equally careless of comfort. In his diary there are entries such as this touching a tramp of twenty miles: "Starting at night in advance, I felt my way along in the dark, partly by the sensation of a trodden path and partly by the stars, knowing our course to be west by north. After a nine miles' walk I lay down, but found the road unusually hard, and was constantly awakened by the guard passing with the baggage, who must have thought me either dead or sick. . . . . I rose from an extemporised bed at four in the morning."

And again, writing from the Bolan Pass: "As we ascended . . . . we were horrified by seeing the bodies of several bullock-drivers who had perished the previous night, and of a dozen or more bullocks which had shared their fate. The violence of the wind as it swept down the narrow ravines and carried dust and grit into our faces, was almost irresistible by man and beast. It took me three hours to walk four miles against it one evening after sunset, and some natives who accompanied me gave in and sat shivering under the rocks, and were not brought in till after midnight."

Agreeably with all his views of life, Gordon's exclamation, when he found himself with the besieged garrison at Kandahar, was: "How fortunate I am to be here where I can be of some use!" Equally characteristic of the man was the will by which Gordon left much of his means to the Church Missionary Society for the support of the work he had begun.

To fear Gordon was as complete a stranger as to self-indulgence. The committee at home cautioned him against exposing himself in Afghanistan; but Gordon never counted the possible cost of an effort to reach the people. Of the fanatical Ghazis, whom he wrote down as "one great barrier to missionary work and friendly intercourse with the people," he speaks in friendly terms. Whilst recording the murderous deeds of these ascetics and the punishments which fell upon criminals taken red-handed, he offers an apology for them, as persons "one cannot help pitying," because they "firmly believe they are doing service to God and their country." Whilst planning future work at Kandahar, he admits that he is there at the risk of his life. Yet where other Europeans could not venture alone, Gordon went in safety. He spent hours in the city discussing with *maulvis*, when the authorities deemed his life in danger, and at last threatened him with compulsory return to India.

Gordon himself has reminded us how closely the native observes the European, and it was inevitable that an Englishman who did not live like an Englishman should be the subject of the closest scrutiny. But Gordon could bear this, and on one occasion the most curious testimony was borne to the silent power of this life. A certain *sowar* was great at Bilochi and other frontier tongues; Gordon, wishing to have him as a native teacher, offered high pay and compensation for the loss of pension.

"Sahib," said the man, "I dare not. I should be made a Christian."

Gordon promised that there should be no talk of religion.

"I love Gordon Sahib," was the answer, "and in spite of myself, I am sure I could not help accepting his religion."

The life which speaks with eloquence so persuasive is rarer than we could wish.

Gordon was but forty-one when he fell at Kandahar. A single line upon the family tablet in Hadlow Churchyard summarises the history of his manhood:

"And he left all, rose up, and followed Him."

THE MEN WHO DIED AT LOKOJA

G

THE MEN WHO DIED AT LOKOJA

ON June 25th, 1891, there died at Lokoja on the river Niger, the Rev. John Alfred Robinson. On March 5th, 1892, at the same place, there died Mr. Graham Wilmot Brooke. They fell in an attempt to pierce the Sûdan from its western side; an attempt upon which the shadow of failure seems at present to rest, but an attempt attended with so much encouragement that eventual success cannot be doubted. Indeed, the first steps towards a renewal of the work are already being taken.

Both were remarkable men, in character and training strongly contrasted, but one in zeal for the same cause and fidelity to the same Master.

John Alfred Robinson—born in a family which has many sons in holy orders, the most eminent being Professor Armitage Robinson, of Cambridge

—graduated at Cambridge in 1881, taking a first-class in the theological school. He first volunteered for the mission-field in 1886. Graham Wilmot Brooke, who died at the age of twenty-seven, was a young layman of means, originally educated for the army, who had been led to desire a share in the evangelisation of the Sûdan by the influence of General Gordon.

For the purposes of these pages it is needless to recall the general history of Christian missions on the river Niger. The almost unique personality of the black bishop, Crowther, long gave them peculiar interest in the eyes of English people. Nor is it necessary to do more than mention the differences of opinion in regard to the administration of the Niger mission which long occasioned so much anxiety to the Church Missionary Society and its friends. Here I wish only to speak of the attempt on the Sûdan which will always be associated with the names of J. A. Robinson and Graham Wilmot Brooke.

The two men were, in different ways, admirably suited for their task. Mr. Robinson was a scholar, who brought a trained intellect to bear upon the task of setting the claims of Christ Jesus before the Mohammedans of the Niger Sûdan. The linguistic and translational part of the work was that upon which his interest chiefly centred. Mr. Brooke was an evangelist pure and simple, but wholly free from the bondage of conventionality. Each was a distinct and strong personality; but the one fitted into the other. They had the same enthusiasm; they trusted the same methods. Masters of the Hausa language and equipped with some Christian literature in that tongue, they knew that a field of almost unexampled magnitude and interest lay before them. That field was carefully chosen with regard to its linguistic as well as its physical and religious conditions. Mr. Wilmot Brooke made a preliminary survey before committing himself definitely to the work, and the whole scheme was devoid of the haphazard element which has sometimes brought disappointment upon well-intentioned projects.

The Sûdan was the true object of the mission, an area some 3,500 miles by 500, containing a population which has been roughly estimated at 80,000,000. The particular nation upon which it was sought to concentrate attention was that of the Hausas, a people distinguished alike in war and in commerce, yet hardly pressed by sterner nations—the Arabs and the Fulas. By nature intelligent, courteous, accessible, and industrious, they invite the labours of the evangelist, more especially as they only accepted Mohammedanism at the point of the sword, and follow it with no enthusiasm. Their language is spoken by some 15,000,000 of people, of whom, perhaps, 300,000 read and write it in the Arabic character.

The principles upon which the work was to be carried on were modern, yet also very ancient. Given health, the literary part of the undertaking was only a question of time; but active evangelistic work in the crowded towns and villages within reach of those who made Lokoja their centre was not so easy. It seemed to these pioneers that it was impossible to expect open doors if the missionaries went as British subjects, with the shadowy but still threatening power of Great Britain behind them. They resolved, therefore, as

George Maxwell Gordon did in the Punjab, to sink, as far as possible, the European; to use native dress and native food; to lay aside any claims which Englishmen might have upon the protection of their country's flag, and to tender formal submission to native rulers amongst whose subjects they preached. This seemed to them the best protection against native fanaticism, and the best means of securing freedom from the restraint which the civil power likes to exercise over missionary enterprise where there are signs that a breach of the peace may ensue.

It was at first thought that on these plans work amongst the Hausas might be carried on with fewer disadvantages than were met with in other African missions at a distance from the coast. The life of the people was such that Europeans might, without serious difficulty, follow native habits in regard to house, food, and clothing. Transport was simplified, for the Niger provided a great highway. The climate even was recommended as less perilous than on the delta of the Niger or in any other African missions. But in this last particular, as we shall presently see, the forecasts were conspicuously falsified by events.

The centre of the work was to be Lokoja, a town lying at the junction of the Niger and the Binué, some 300 miles from the sea. Its population was comparatively small—only about 3,000; but it was an admirable centre, commanding the two great rivers, focussing much of the trade of the district, bringing together men from all the surrounding tribes, and enjoying a secured peace from the presence of the Royal Niger Company. Many years before this there had been at Lokoja a model farm, the circumstances of which suggested to Dickens the "Borioboola Gha" of "Bleak House." There was still a native congregation there, but it was not the fruits of missionary enterprise amongst the people around.

The plans complete and a little body of workers secured, Mr. Robinson left first for the field. Shortly afterwards, on January 20th, 1890, farewell was taken of the others at Exeter Hall. Mr. Wilmot Brooke and his wife, the Rev. Eric Lewis and his sister, and Dr. C. F. Harford-Battersby were in this company.

On April 4th the party reached Lokoja. They found the Christian congregation to number about a hundred, chiefly formed of African immigrants from Sierra Leone and native servants of the Royal Niger Company. The spiritual life of that congregation was burning low, and its example was not salutary. But without delay the mission party settled down to work. The congregation was taken in hand; translational work systematically pursued; the hospital worked by Dr. Harford-Battersby; visiting, nursing, and the instruction of Christian adherents committed to the ladies. Thus the Sûdan mission began its task without a shadow even of the tragic element so early apparent in the life of the Nyanza mission, on the other side of Africa.

At the end of six months Mr. Robinson had, however, a chequered story to tell. The spiritual life of the old congregation, which was not missionary in its constitution, had been renewed under measures of discipline and under personal pleading such as are too rarely employed in congregations at home. The use of native dress had been found helpful with the people and a comfort to the wearers. On an early advance up the Niger the population had welcomed the change, and cried: "Ah, that is a sensible dress for this country. Now we know that you really want to come near us." Native food had been used without inconvenience or harm. The medical work had proceeded steadily, making, as it always does, an entrance for the evangelist into many homes which might otherwise be closed. The first baptism was that of a Mohammedan patient in the hospital. The workers had found the language easier than they had ventured to expect; but saw reason to believe that little could be done in the interior until they had at least one Gospel printed in idiomatic Hausa.

Sorrow, however, had early fallen upon the party. In September Mr. Wilmot Brooke fell ill of typhoid fever, and to save his life returned home for a little while. For a time the diminished European staff devoted itself chiefly to the study of the language; but in January

1891, aggressive work was once more taken up with vigour. Two more ladies, Miss Griffin and Miss Clapton, now arrived as reinforcements. Mr. Lewis and one native helper went off itinerating amongst the villages occupied by the heathen Basas. The tour was marked by no unusual incident, but showed a large field in which evangelistic work was possible. Mr. Lewis was recalled by the news of serious illness amongst the party at Lokoja. A tour of more importance was undertaken by Mr. Robinson and Dr. Harford-Battersby, also accompanied by a native agent. Their destination was Bida, the capital of the Nupé kingdom, a town with some sixty thousand inhabitants. Dr. Harford-Battersby had not long recovered from hæmaturic fever, and felt the heat severely. Upon him the burden of the work fell, with the result that the fever returned. He was carried down to the boat, and thus sent back to Lokoja. There he found Miss Clapton so ill that to remain meant death. Her time of work had been short, but had sufficed to prove her an exceptionally skilful missionary of varied powers and equal activity. Mr. Lewis was also amongst the invalids. He first went down the river to Onitsha for change of air; that failing, he too was driven home.

But a still sorer trial was awaiting the mission. In May considerable brain exhaustion had shown itself in Mr. Robinson, who, for some relief, had handed over to Mr. Brooke the secretaryship of the mission. But just then the presence in Lokoja of a *mallam* of repute and learning offered an unusual opportunity for linguistic inquiry. Into this Mr. Robinson, despite his enfeebled state, plunged with ardour. The result was an alarming attack of what was at first supposed to be hæmaturic fever. But the fever yielded to treatment, and then the real trouble was seen to be brain meningitis. The end speedily drew near. "To the last," wrote his colleague, "he was wonderfully free from acute pain, and quite free from delirium; but on the 25th (of June) his strength sank rapidly, and he became quite calm. Towards midnight, after a long period of quietness, he awakened suddenly and completely, and, with a strong and vigorous voice, called out 'God be praised,' then sinking back, he fell asleep." Mr. Brooke has described his friend's character in terms innocent of flattery:

"Possessed of rare energy of mind and body, and with great power of adapting himself to circumstances, so that he seemed equally at home whether managing a steamer on the delta, or living as a native among natives in Bida; at repairing buildings with his Kru labourers, or at work with his lexicons and concordances in his little room at Lokoja—this mission could never have been started without him; and we never expect to get such a leader or such a companion again."

The loss to the mission was all the greater because Mr. Robinson had taken upon himself the linguistic work without which evangelistic enterprise could hope to leave but ineffectual and transitory impressions. His earnest hope was to give the natives some portions of the Holy Scriptures in the Hausa language, portions so skilfully rendered and so judiciously got up as to have little trace of European handiwork about them. He was the happier in this work because of the ease and charm of his manner with the natives. "He might," says Mr. Lewis, "have been a Hausa born, so perfectly was he at his ease among them; and, what is perhaps more difficult, they were free to come in and sit down at all hours of the day and make themselves perfectly at home, without seriously interrupting work he might have on hand."

The mission, thus weakened, lost another recruit in August, when health compelled the return home of Mr. Roberts. Yet the work never ceased, and from time to time encouragement was forthcoming. But in January a new danger arose. A neighbouring chief threatened Lokoja and attacked its outskirts. Mr. Brooke deemed it best to send the ladies of the mission home, but remained himself to face whatever difficulties might arise. A colleague, Mr. Dobinson, visited him early in the year, and found him full of plans for more evangelistic tours. But a crowning disaster was about to fall.

Mr. Dobinson left Lokoja on February 29th, 1892. Scarcely had he gone when Mr. Brooke was seized with fever, and his condition rapidly became serious. His nurse was Mr. J. J. Williams, a tried and trusted native helper. "I asked," wrote Mr. Williams, "if I should call any of the Europeans here, whom he might tell me of, to come and see him, in case of his getting very serious. He said: 'No, I trust in you. If I should die, bury me in my native dress beside the late Mr. Robinson's grave. If it is difficult to get a coffin, put my body in a native mat, and bury me.'" Mr. Brooke arranged his affairs with the utmost care, and wrote a short inscription for his own grave. It was simplicity itself: the details of family and birth, a single text speaking of the resurrection, and then the record of his missionary work in the words, " Preached Christ in this neighbourhood between July 1889 and February 1892." He died on March 5th.

From the loss of Mr. J. A. Robinson and Mr. Wilmot Brooke the mission has not yet recovered. There are difficulties connected with it into which it is no part of this narrative to enter. But the careers of these two men at least serve as a rebuke to any lightly uttered charges which impugn alike the sincerity and the zeal of the missionary band. Soberly, weighing all things, they planned an incursion into a region hitherto untouched, a region full of peculiar danger. In that attack they persevered whilst others were taken from the field. In that attack they themselves speedily fell. They worked but a little while, yet they cannot have worked in vain.

The memory of Mr. Robinson is kept green at Cambridge by the formation of the Hausa Association to promote the study of that language. The Association has already sent one student to Africa to pursue his linguistic work on the spot. It is an agency which may never win the attention of more than the few, and yet may most vitally affect the future of mission work in the Niger Sûdan.

Printed by BALLANTYNE, HANSON & Co.
London & Edinburgh.

www.ingramcontent.com/pod-product-compliance
Lightning Source LLC
Chambersburg PA
CBHW020142170426
43199CB00010B/855